The Worst

Piss Off

Phenomenal Swear Word To Color

For Stress Releasing

C.J. Willoughby

Happy Coloring!

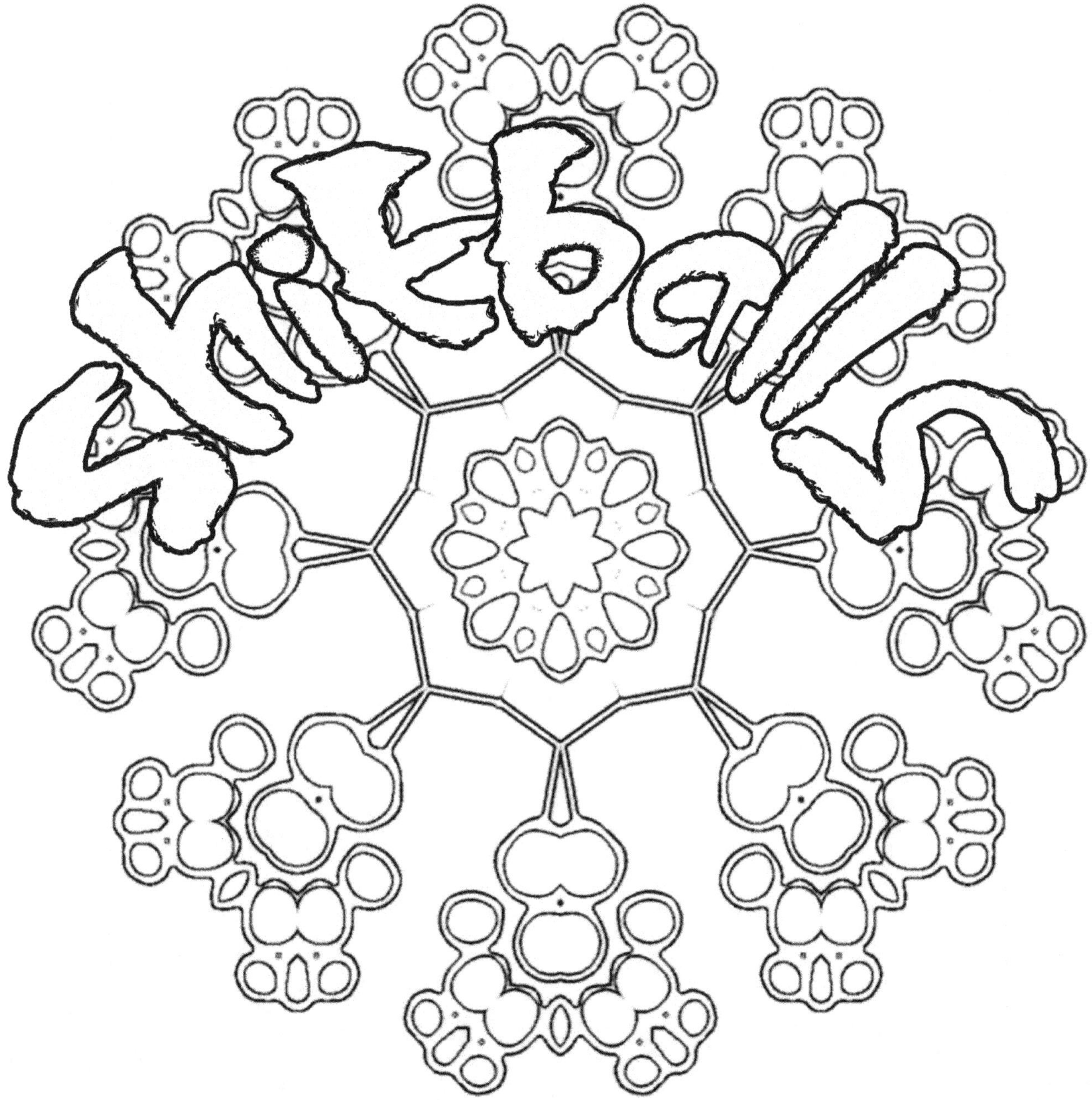
shitballs

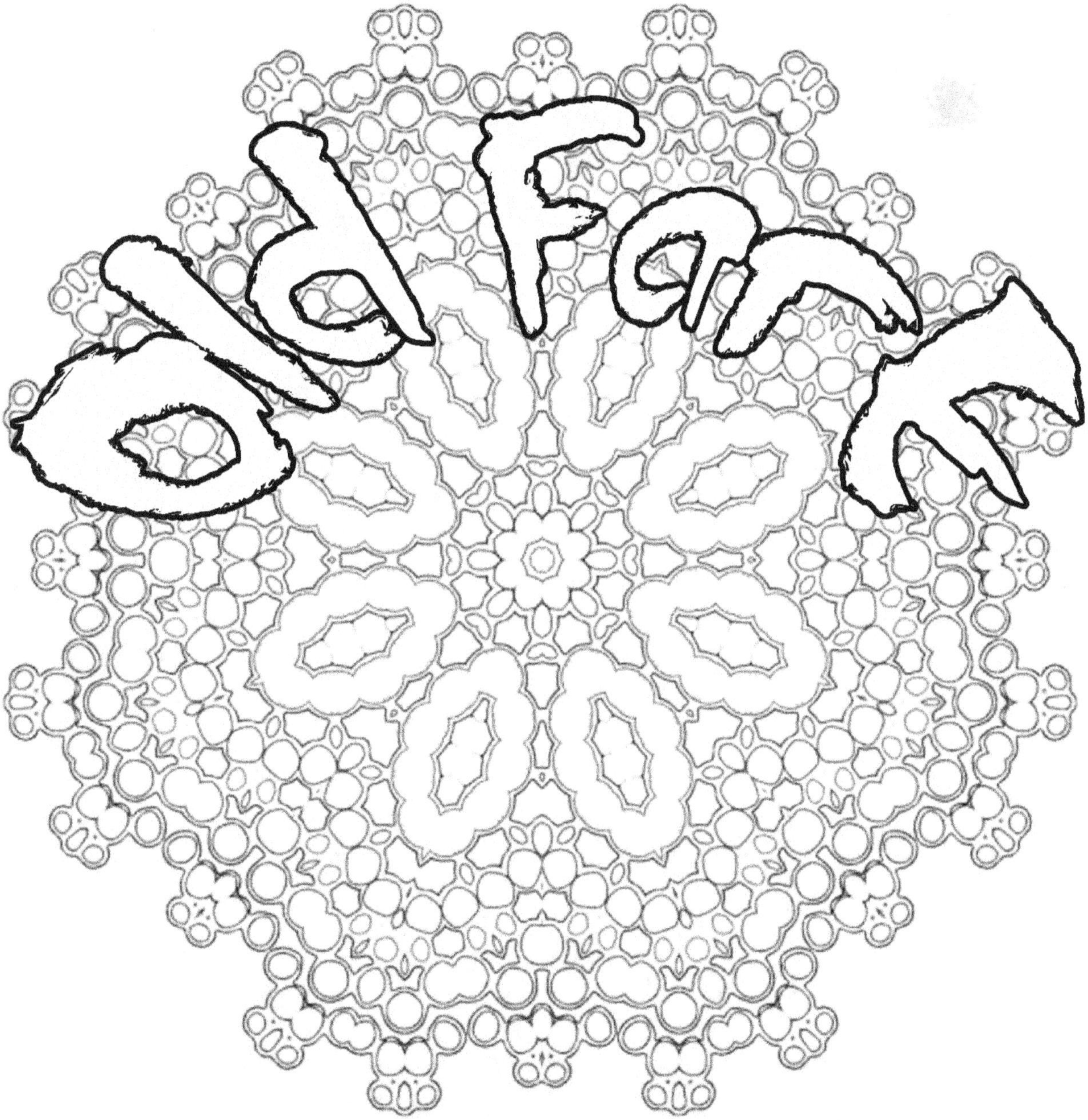
Old Fart

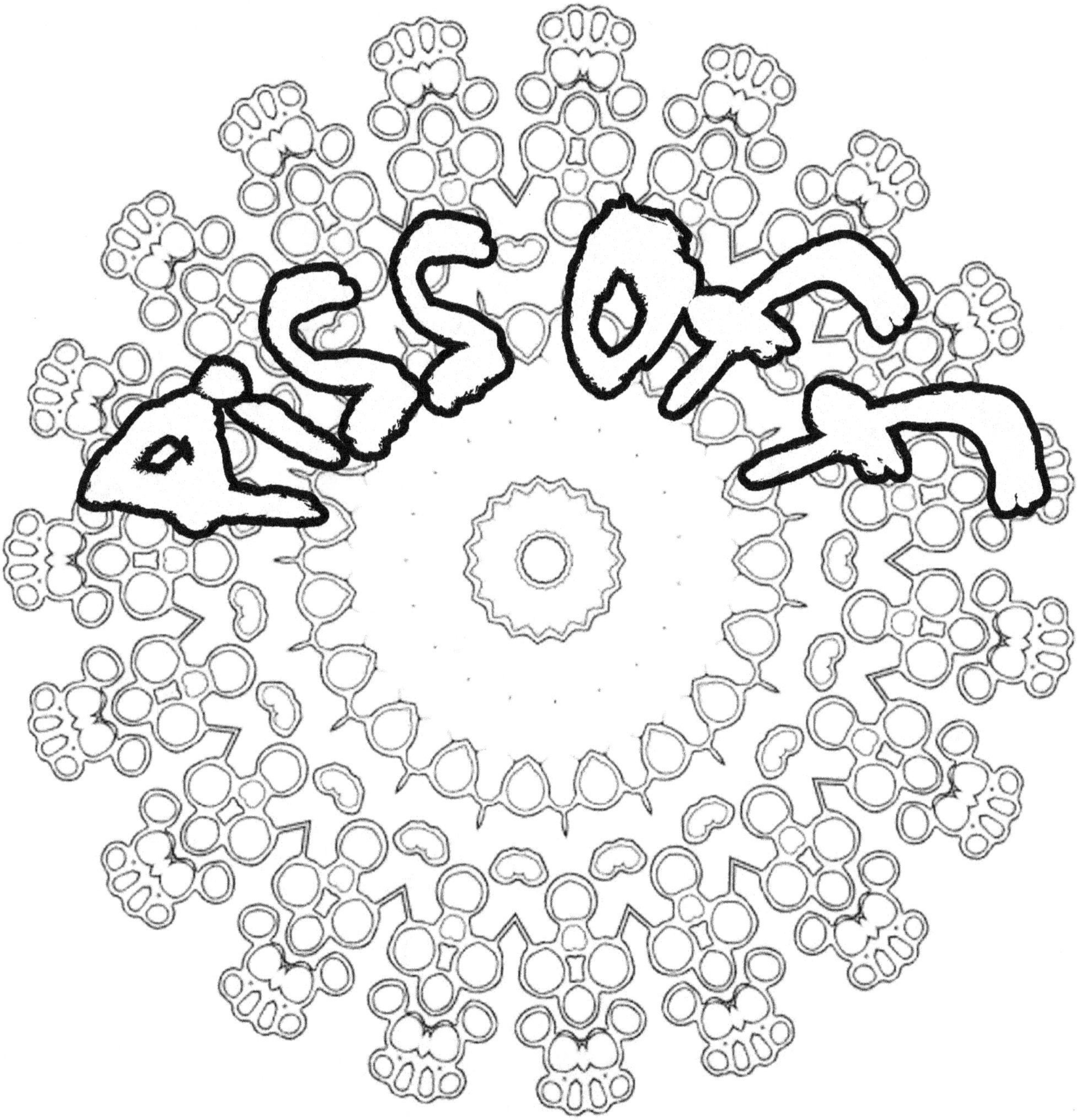
Piss Off

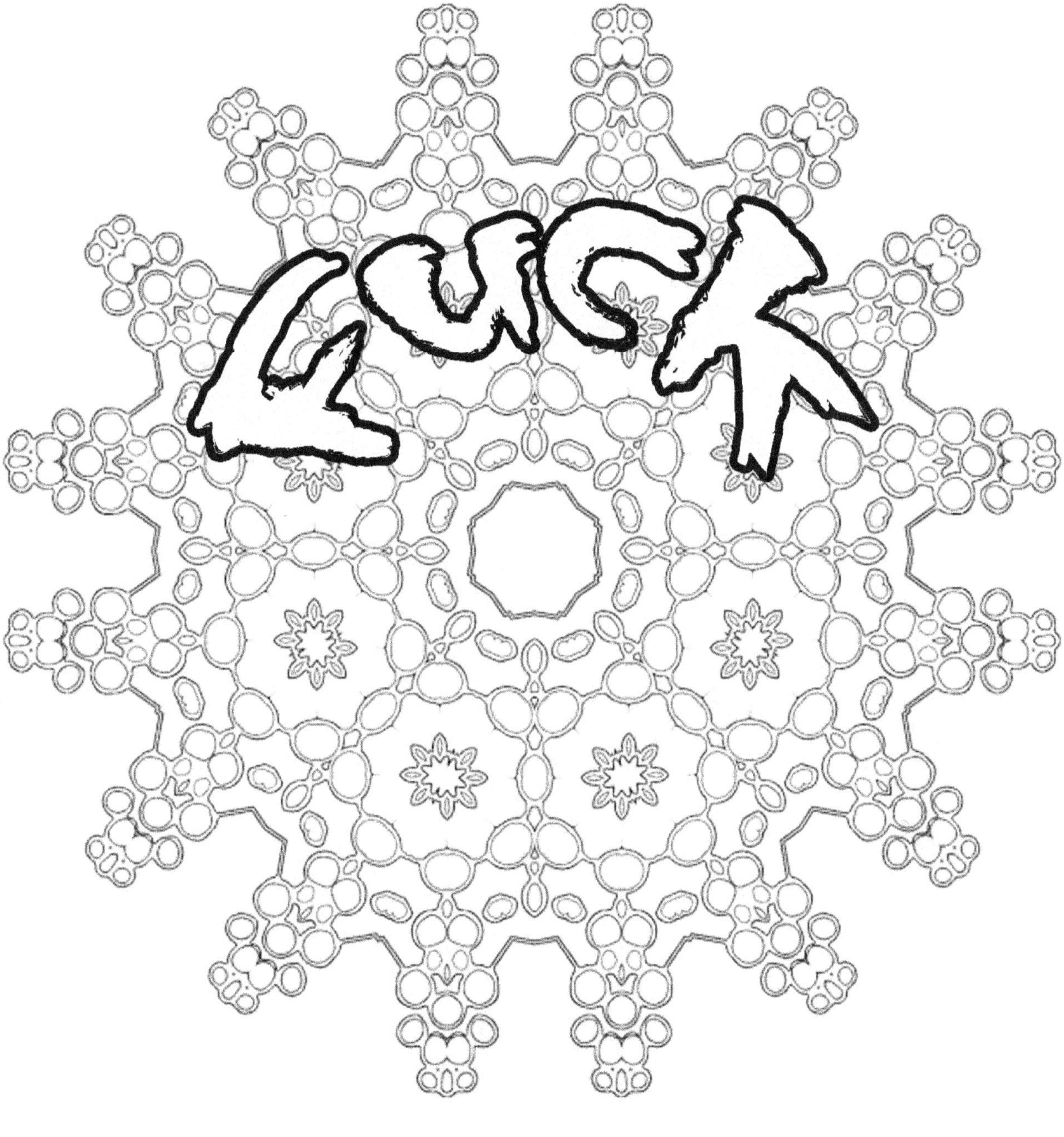
LUCK

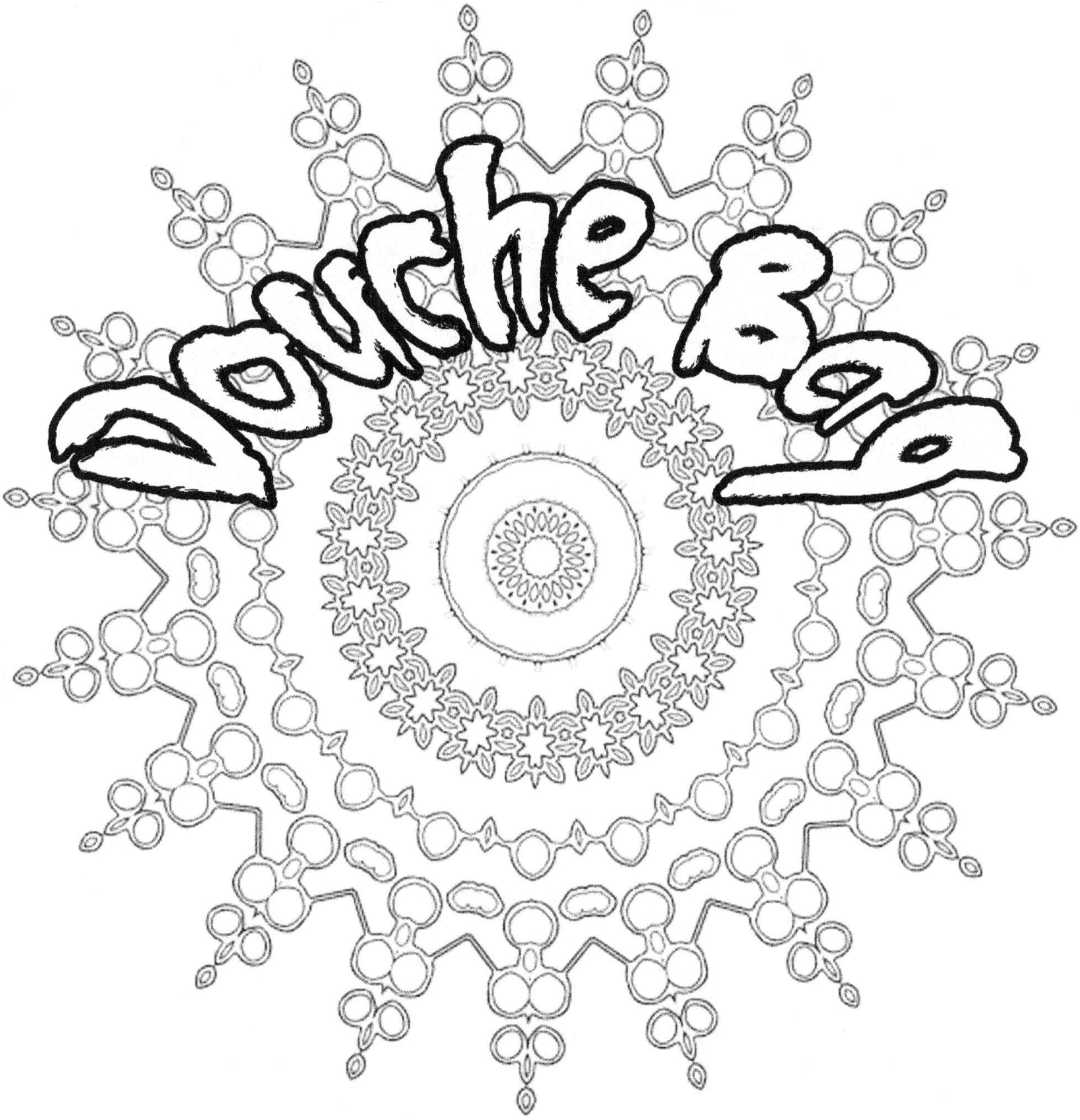
Douche Bag

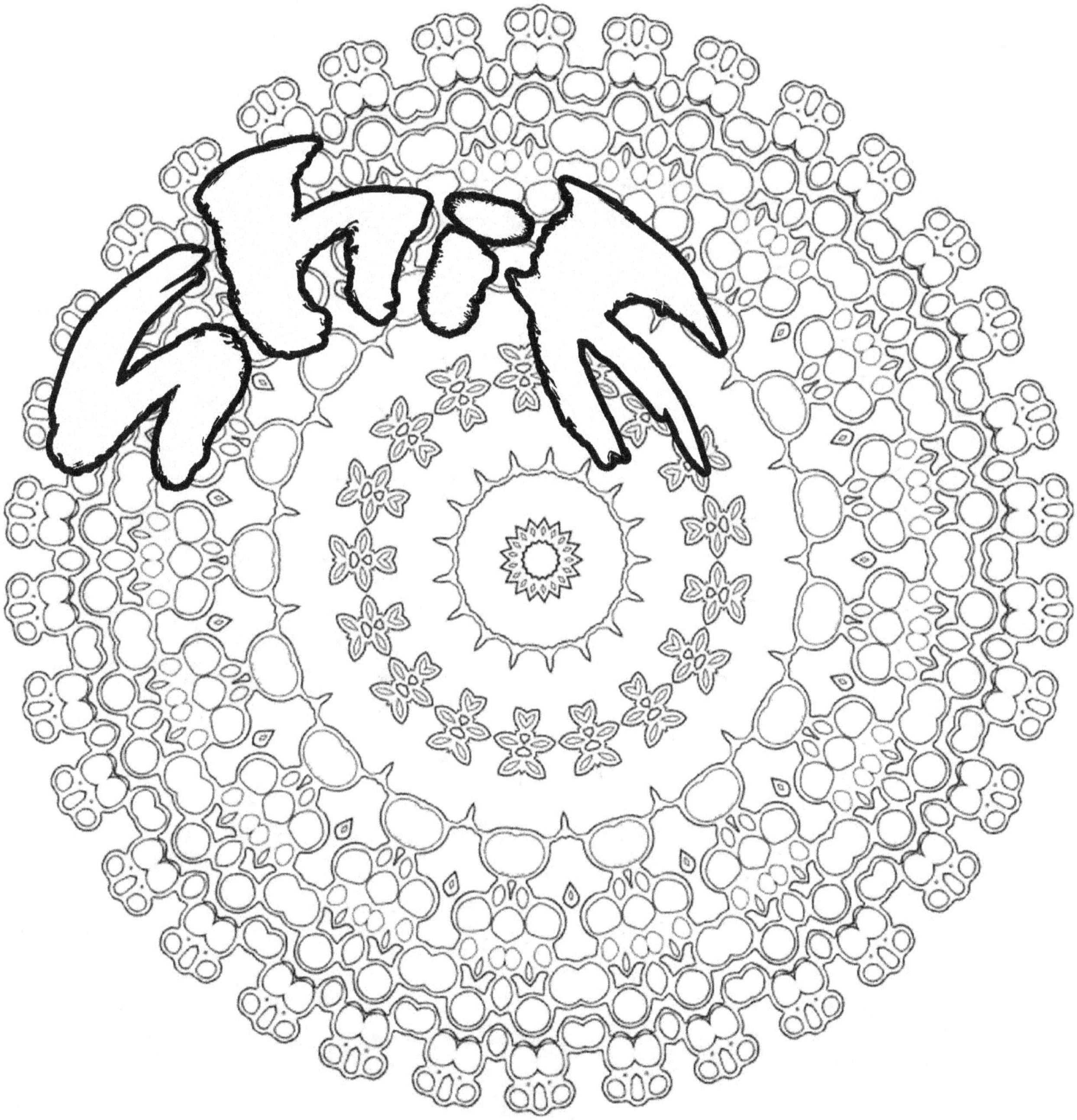
Shit

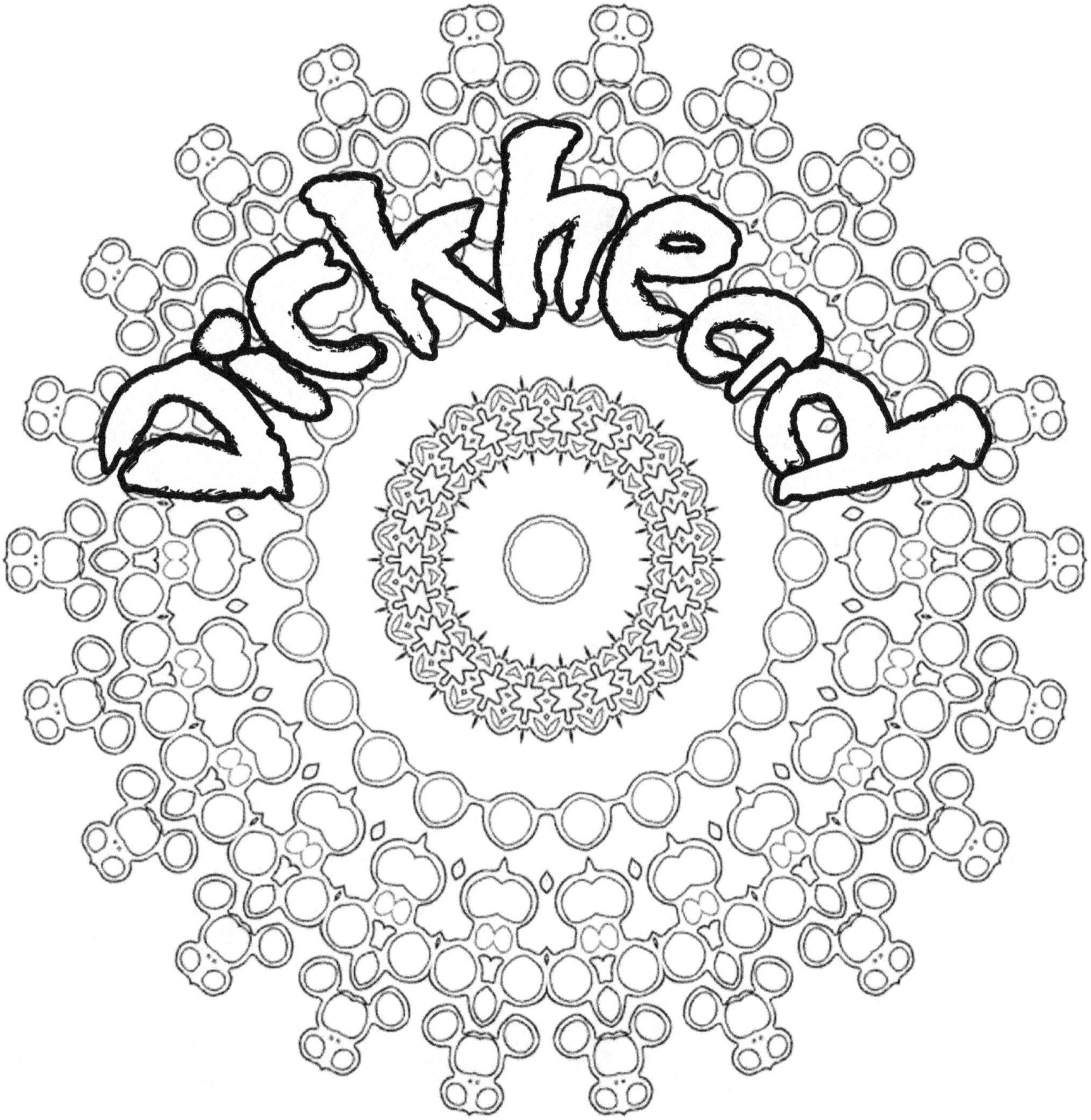
Dickhead

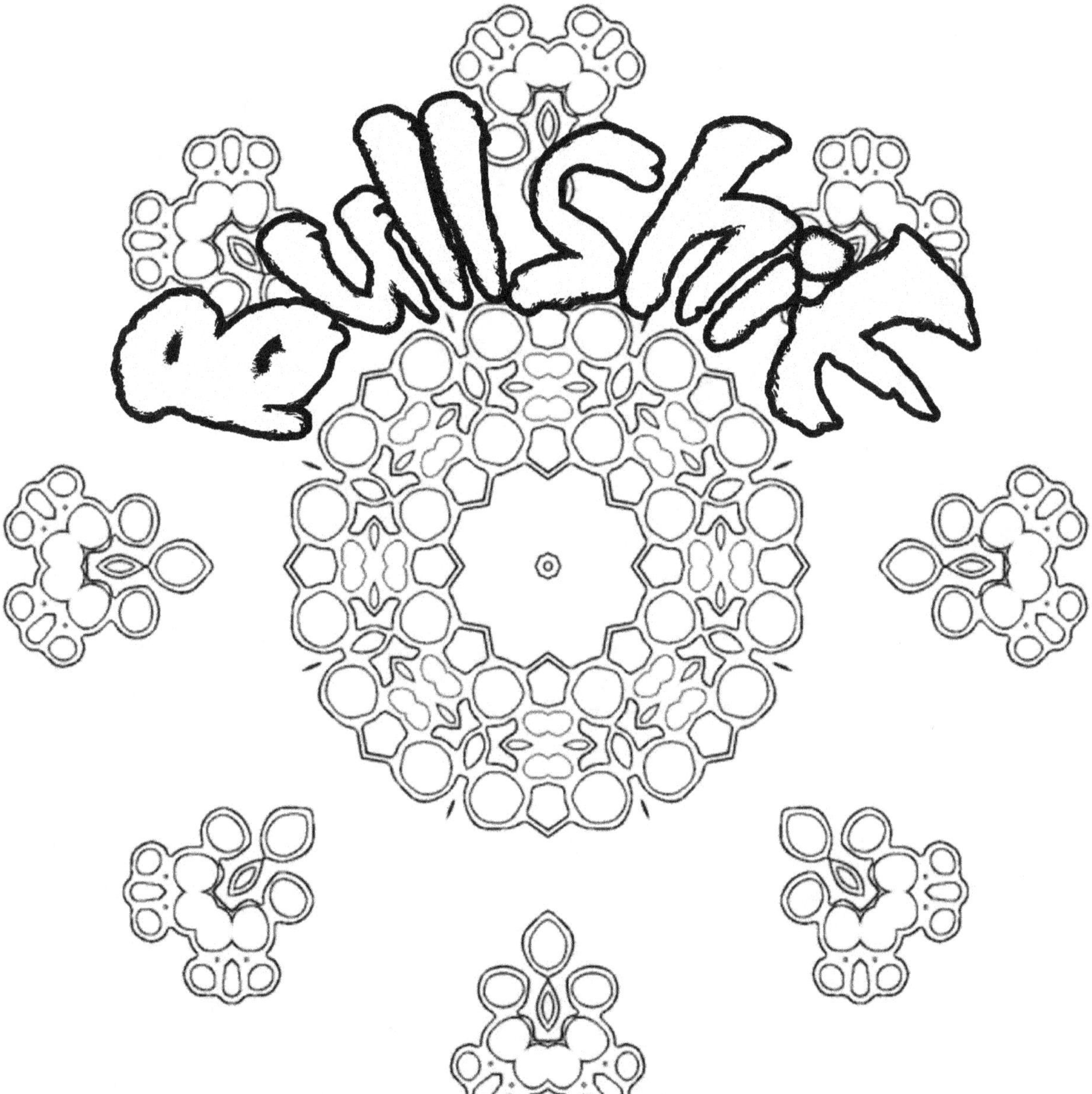
Bullshit

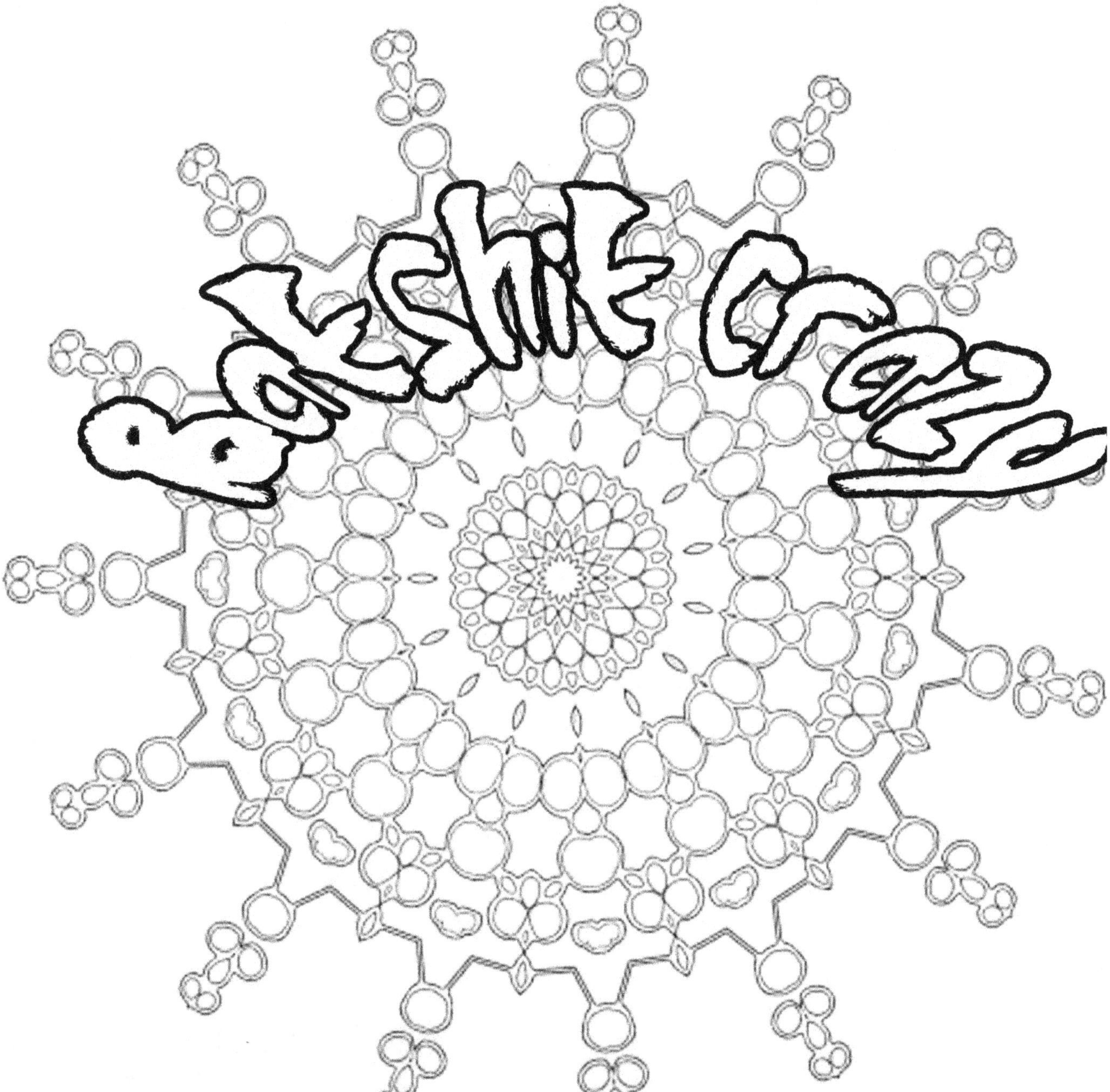
Batshit crazy

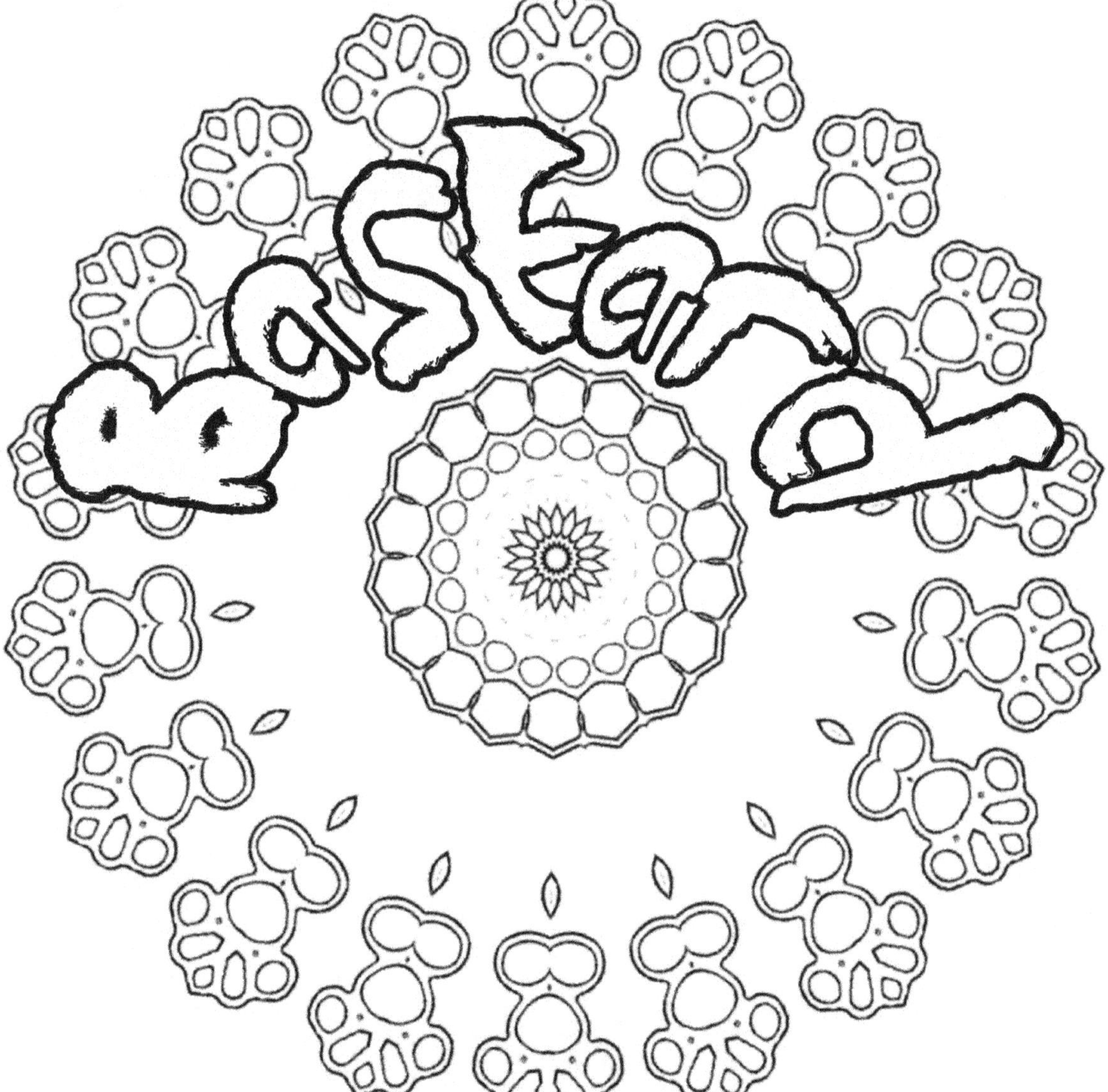
Bastard

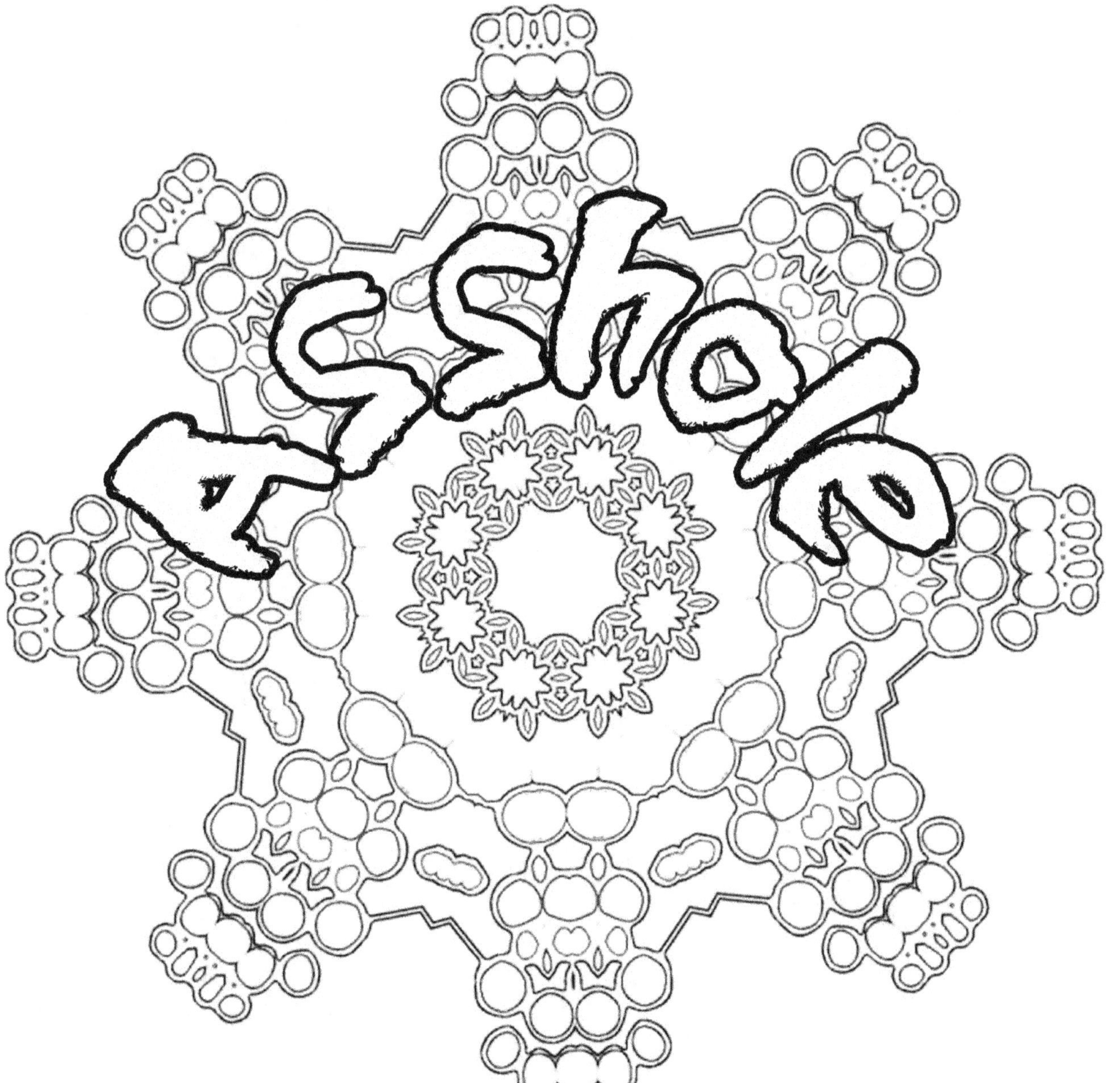
Asshole

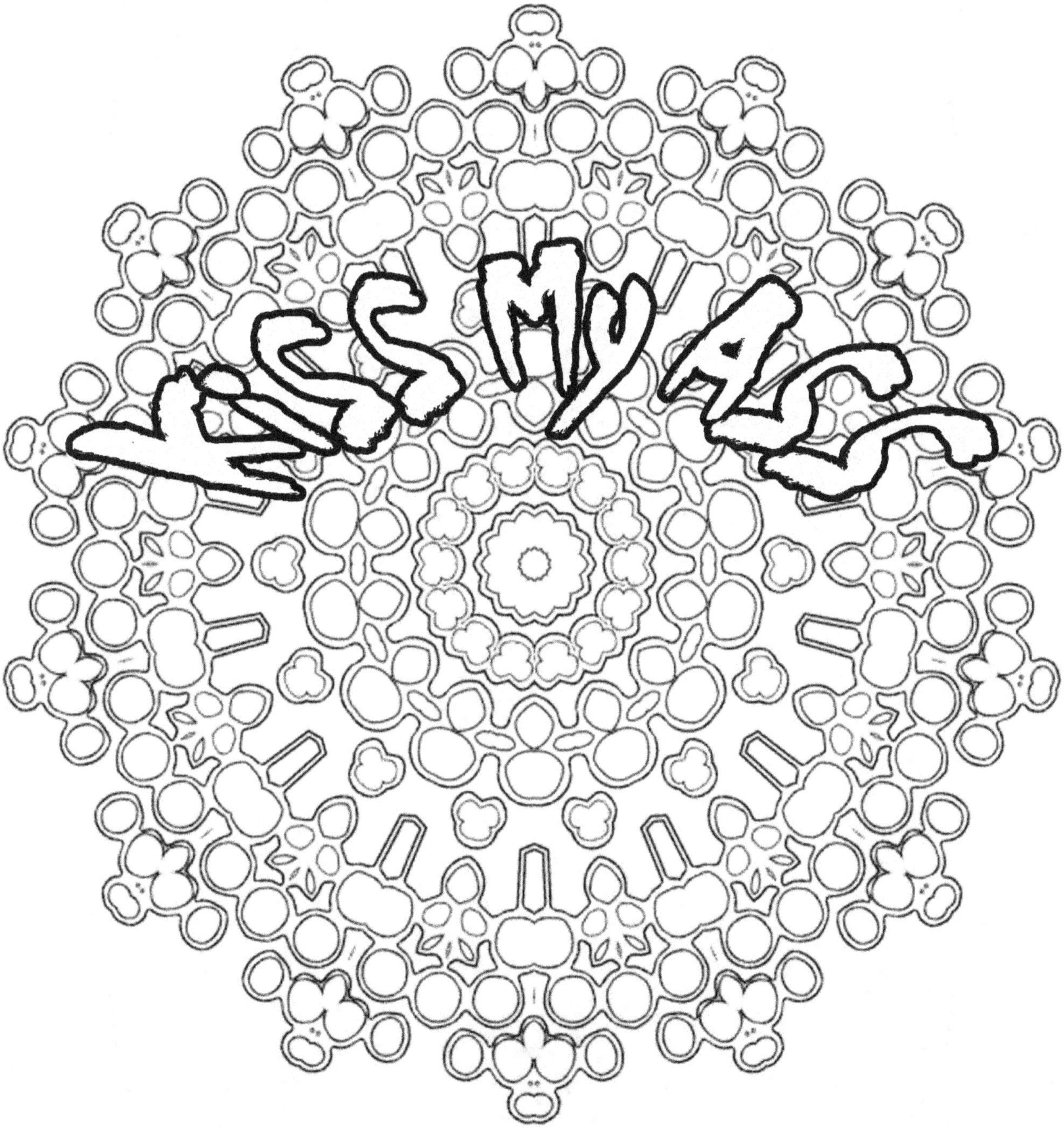
KISS MY ASS

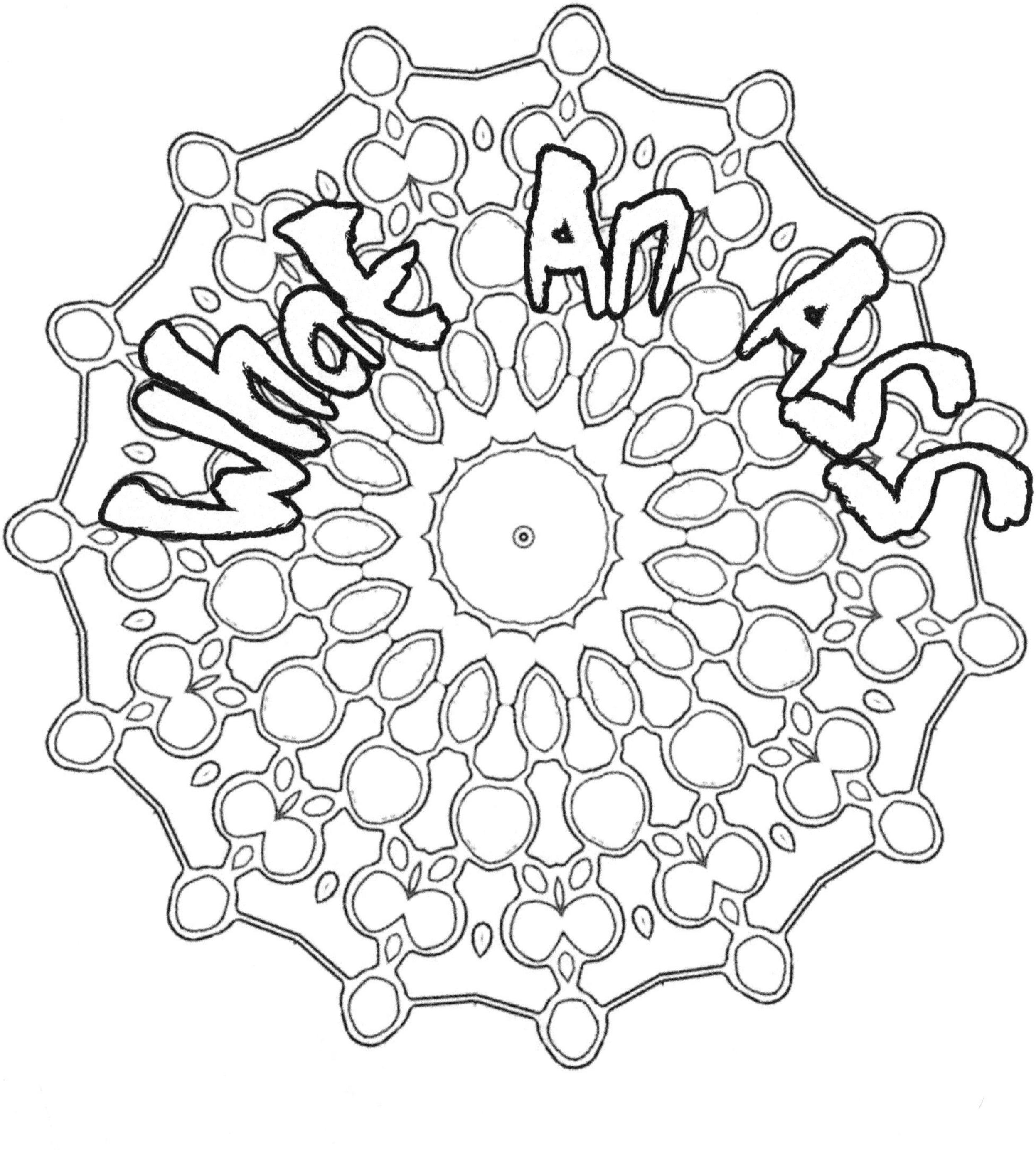
What An Ass

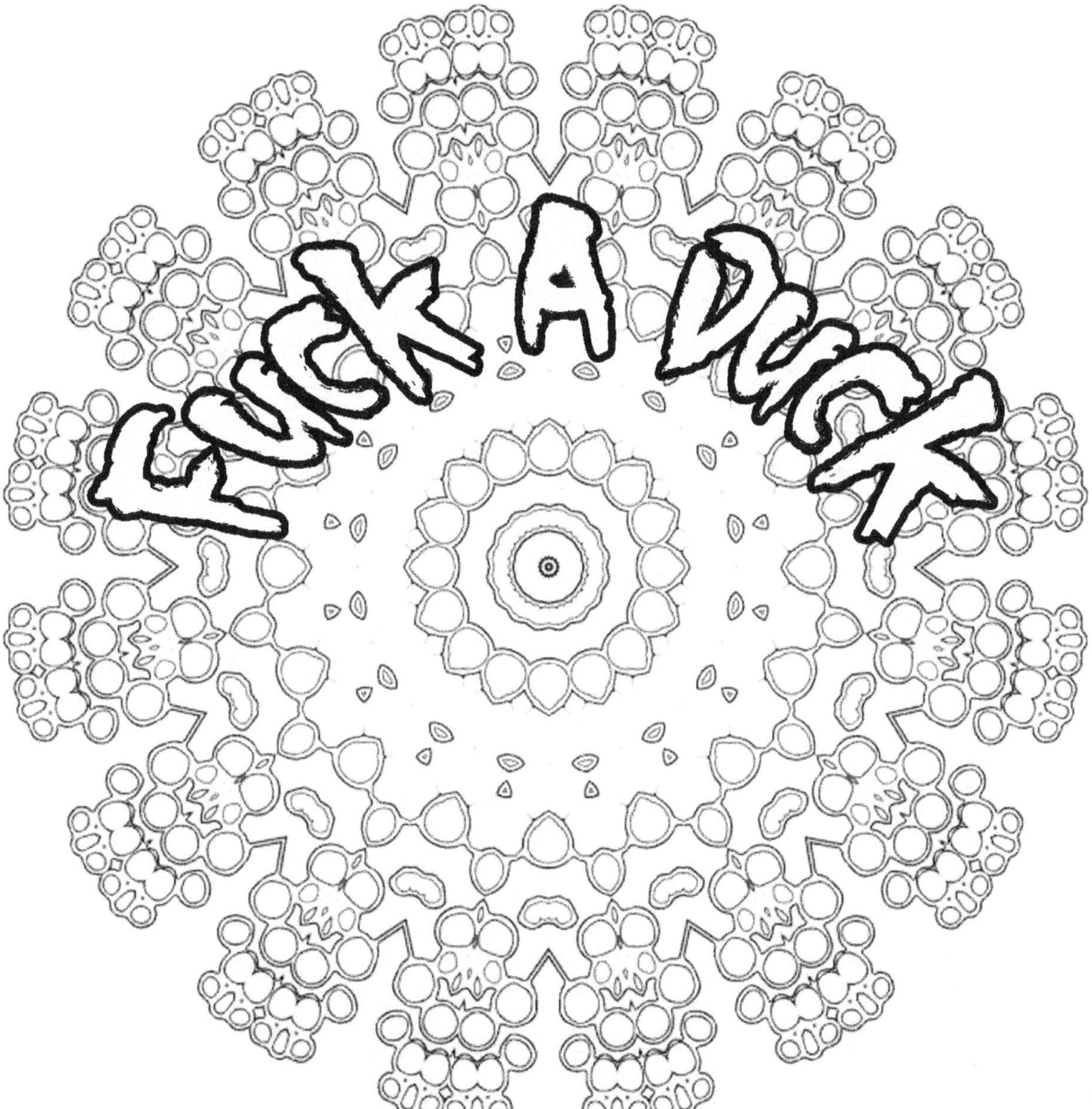
FUCK A DUCK

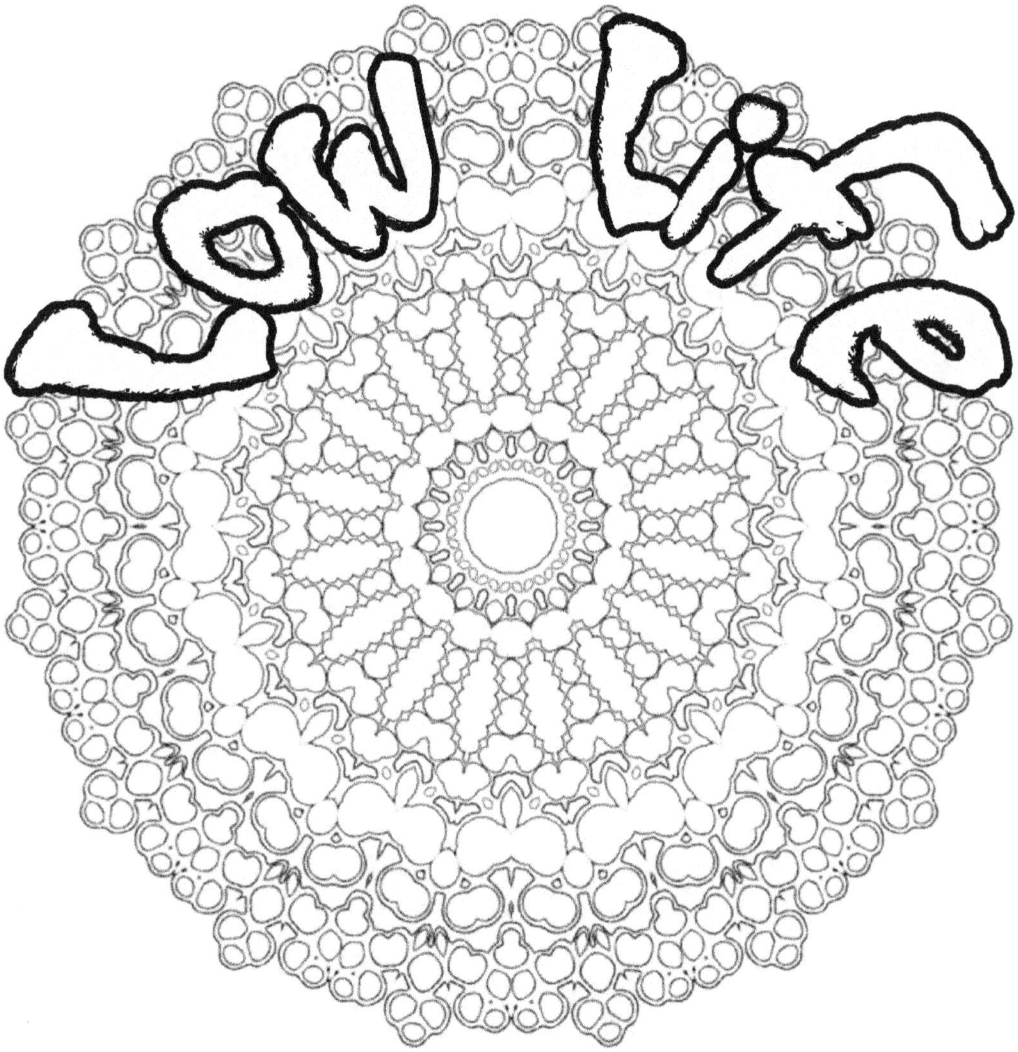
Low Life

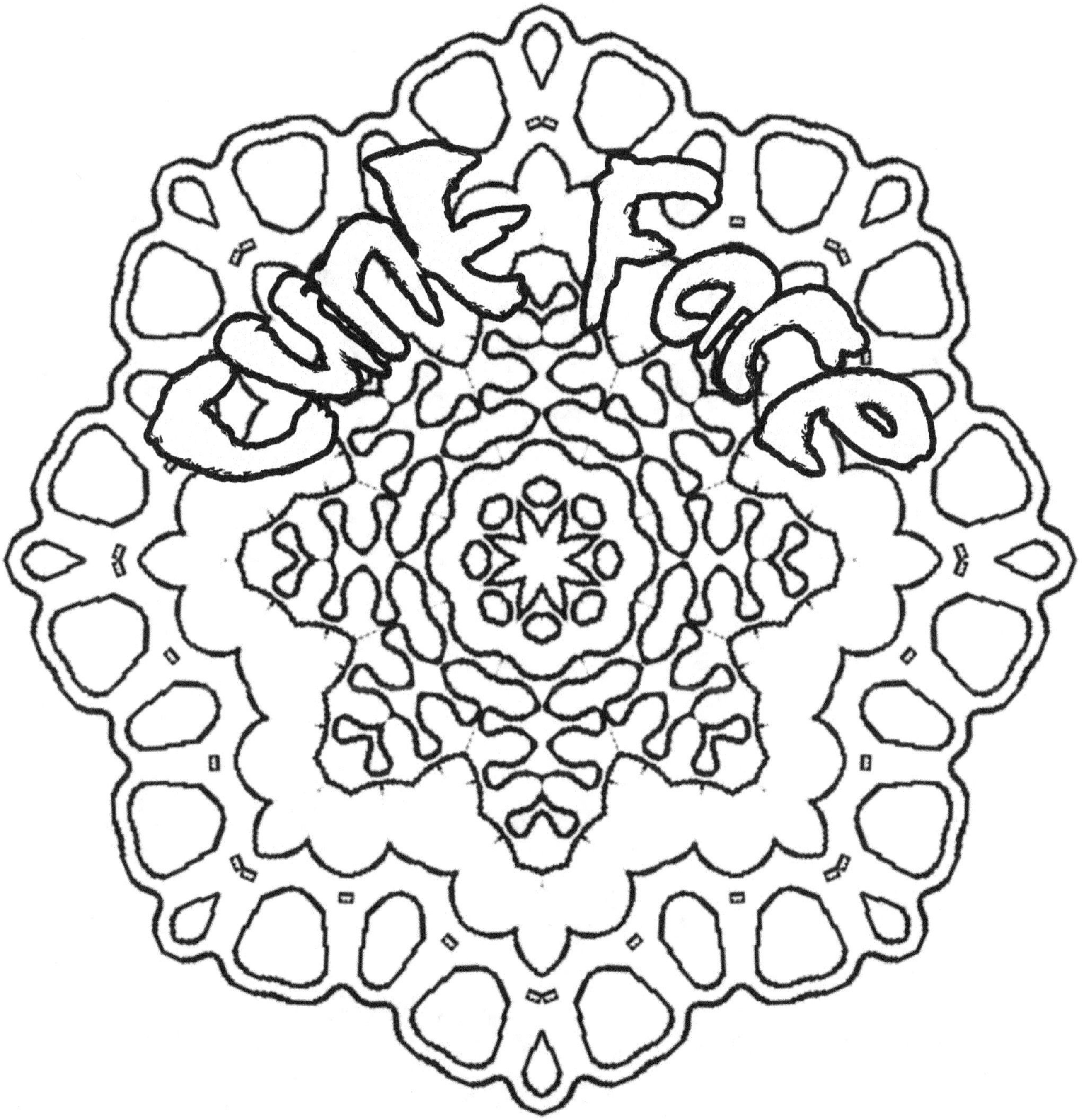
Cunt Face

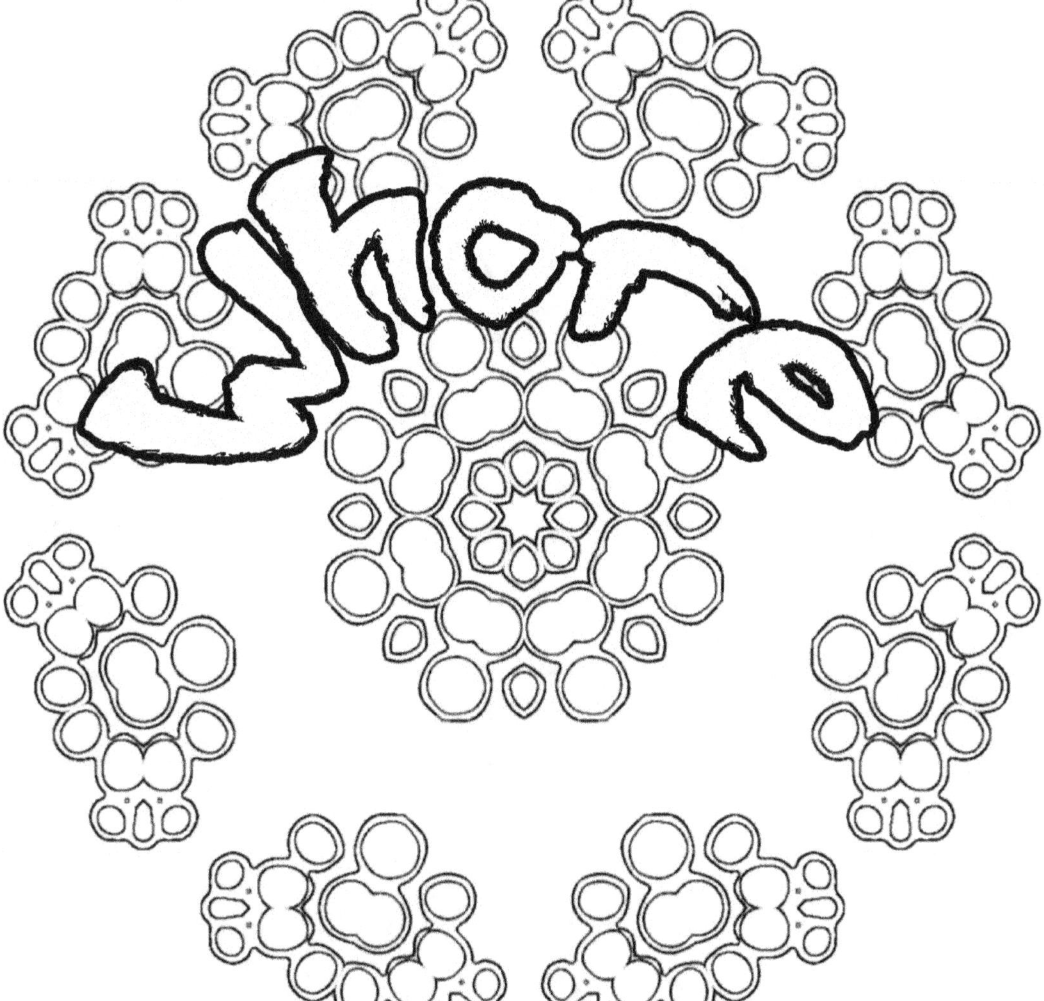
whore

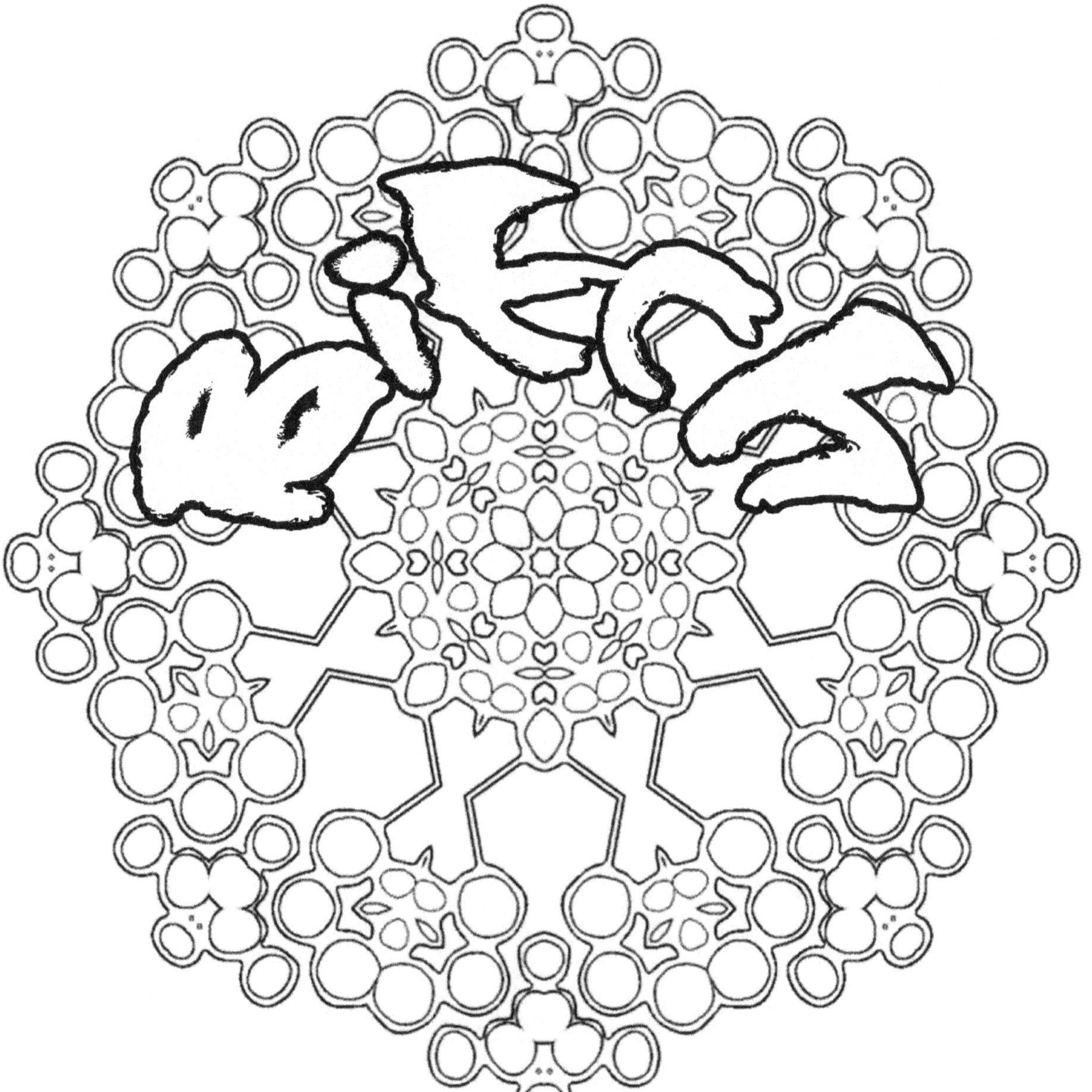

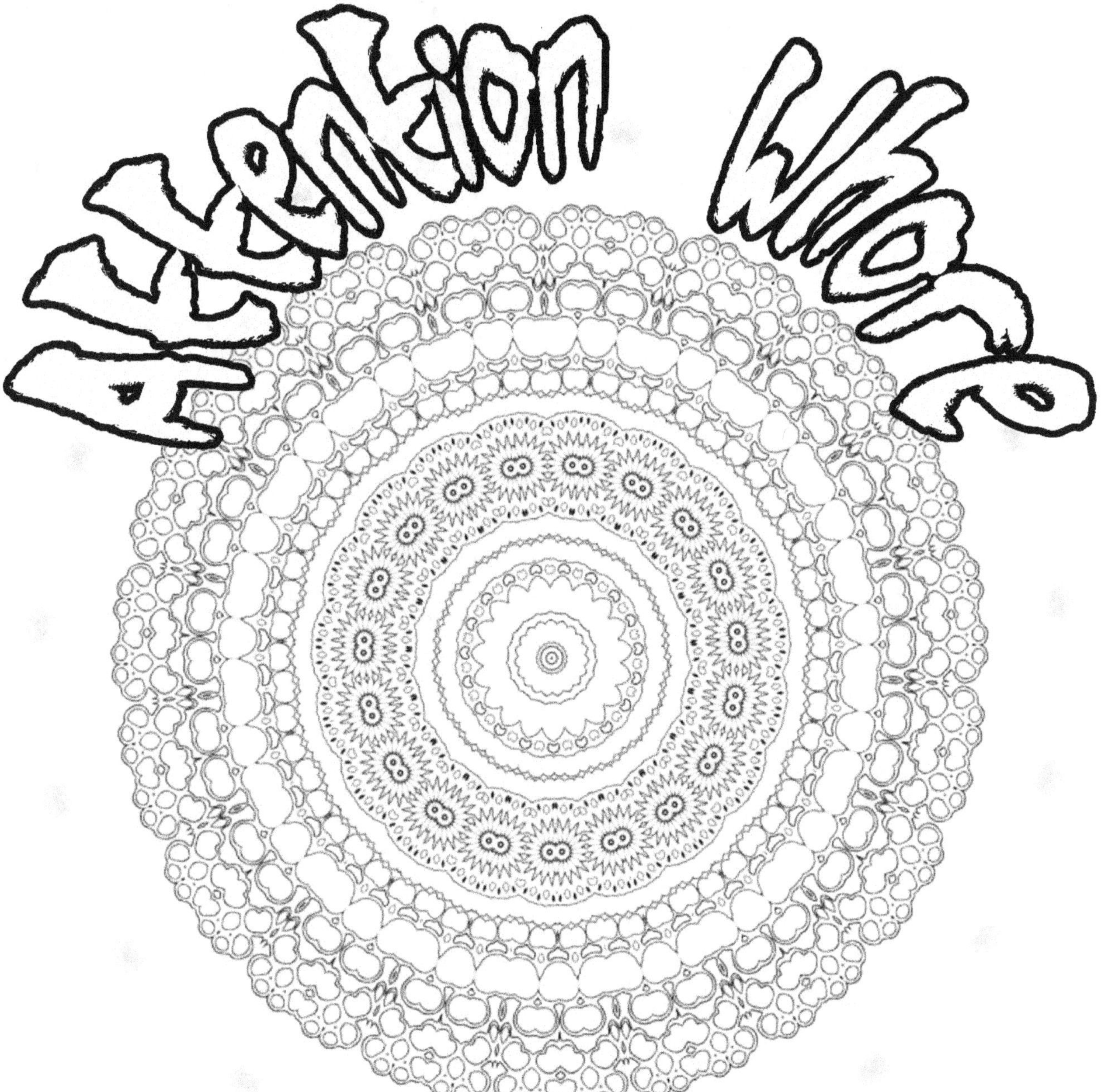
Attention Whore

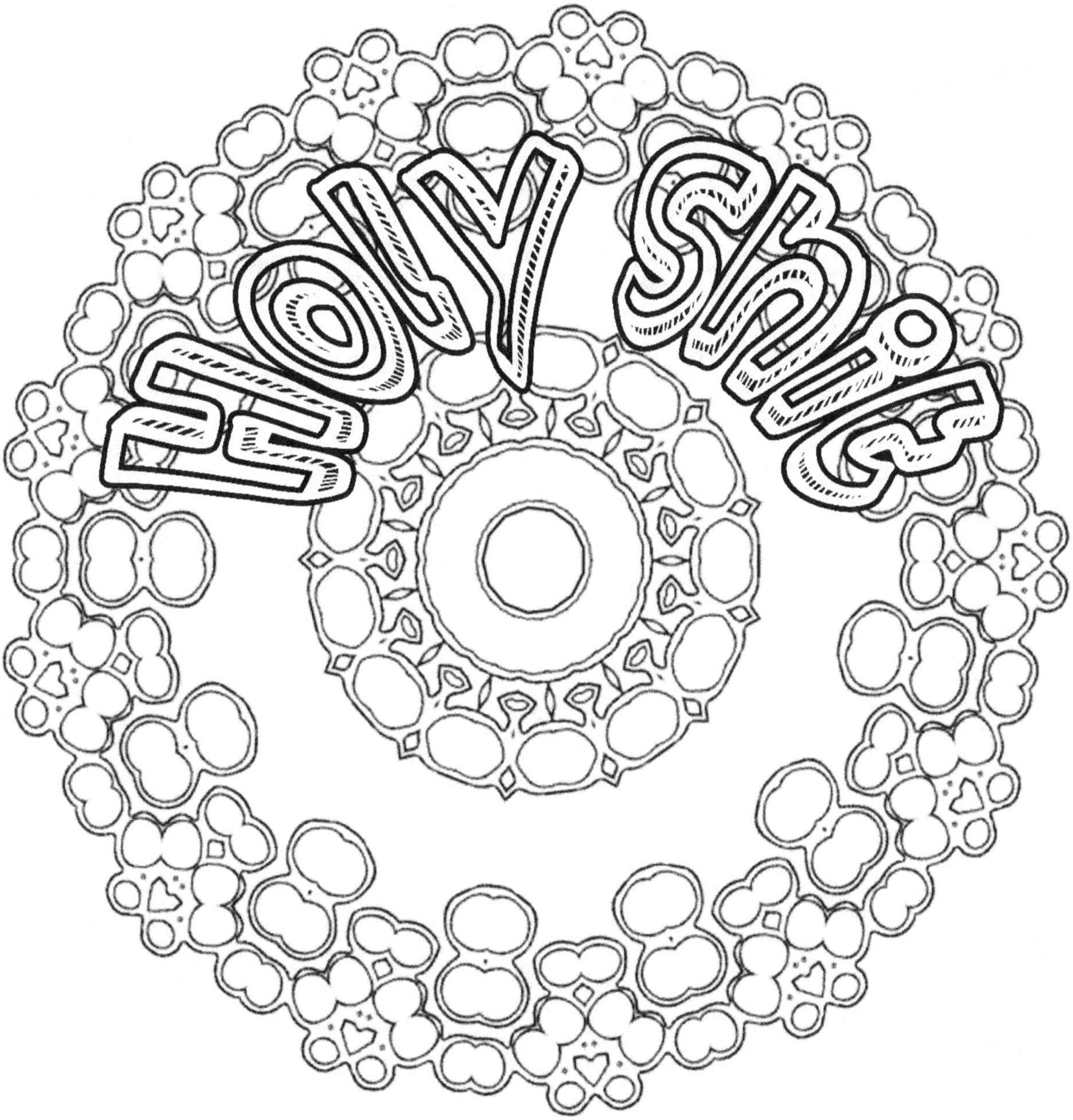
Holy Shit

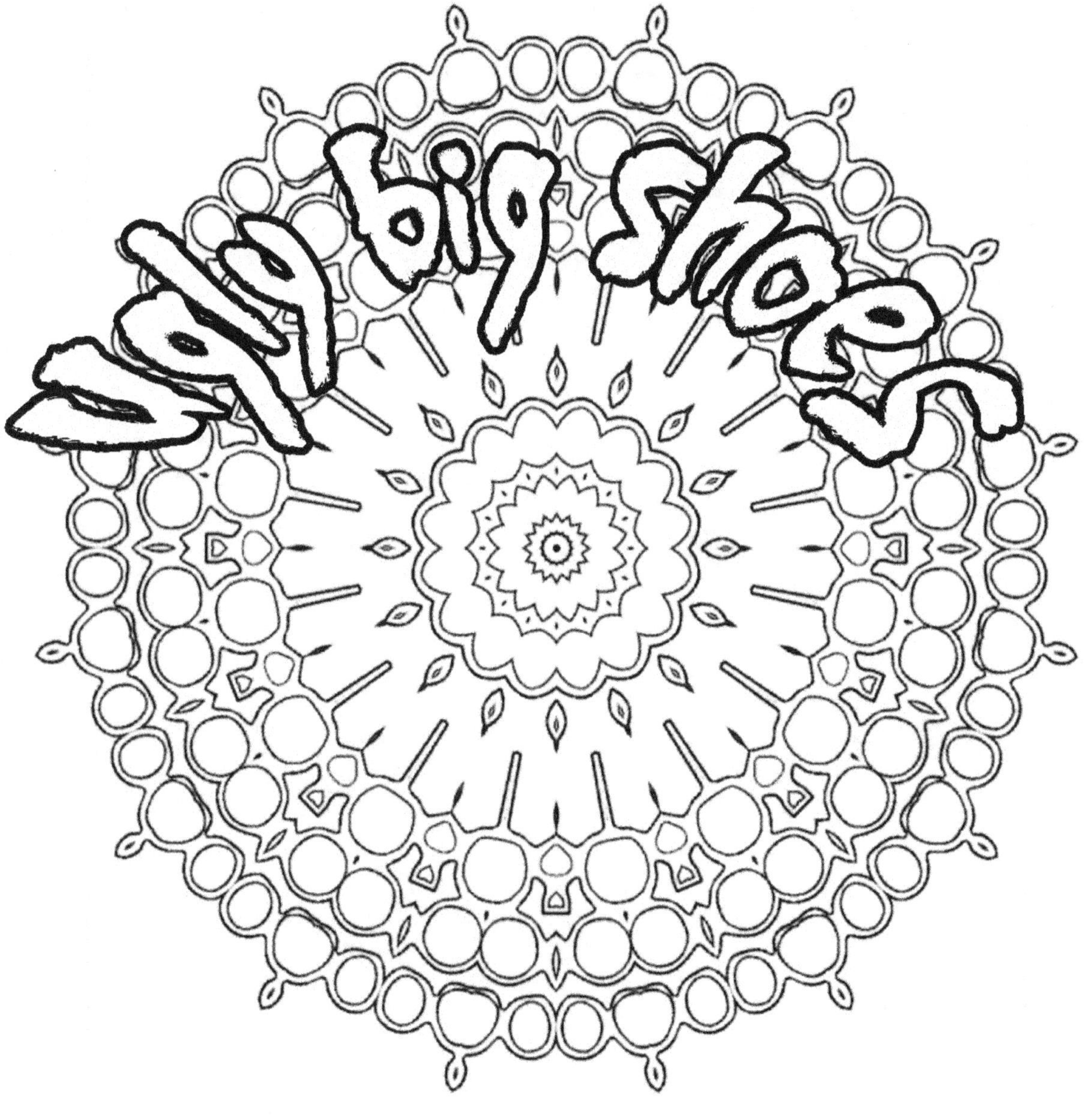
very big shoes

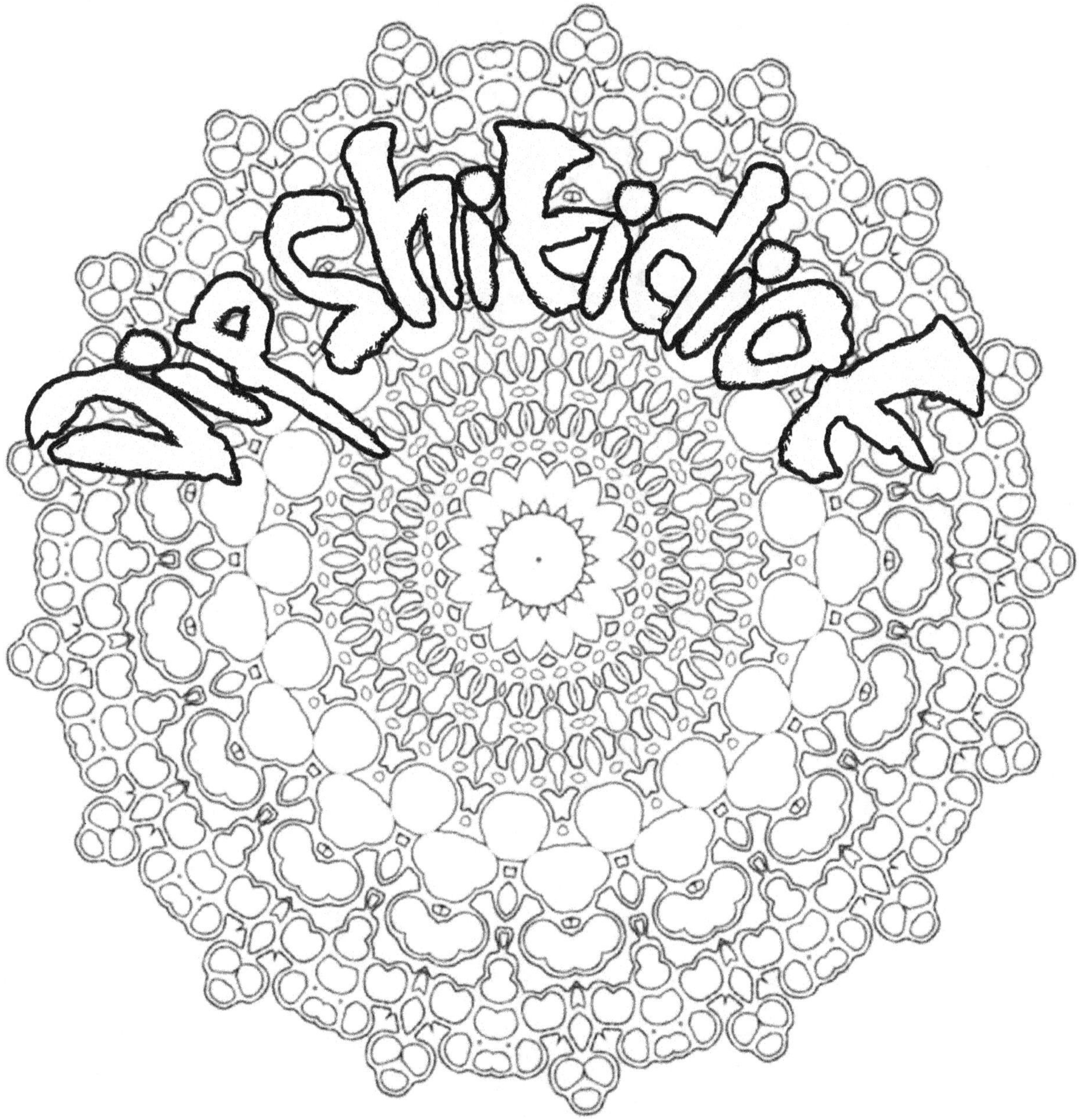
dipshitidiot

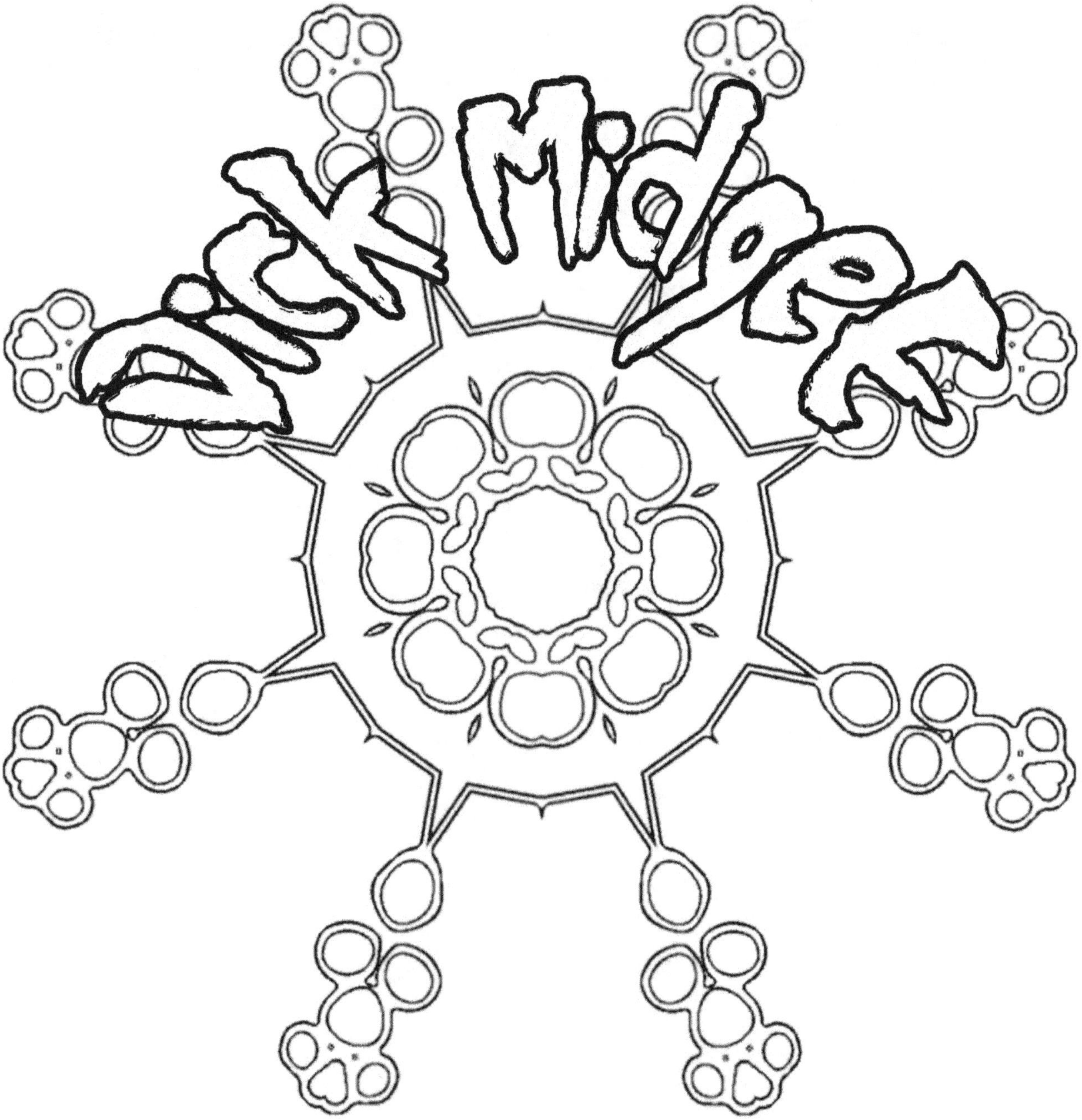
Dick Midget

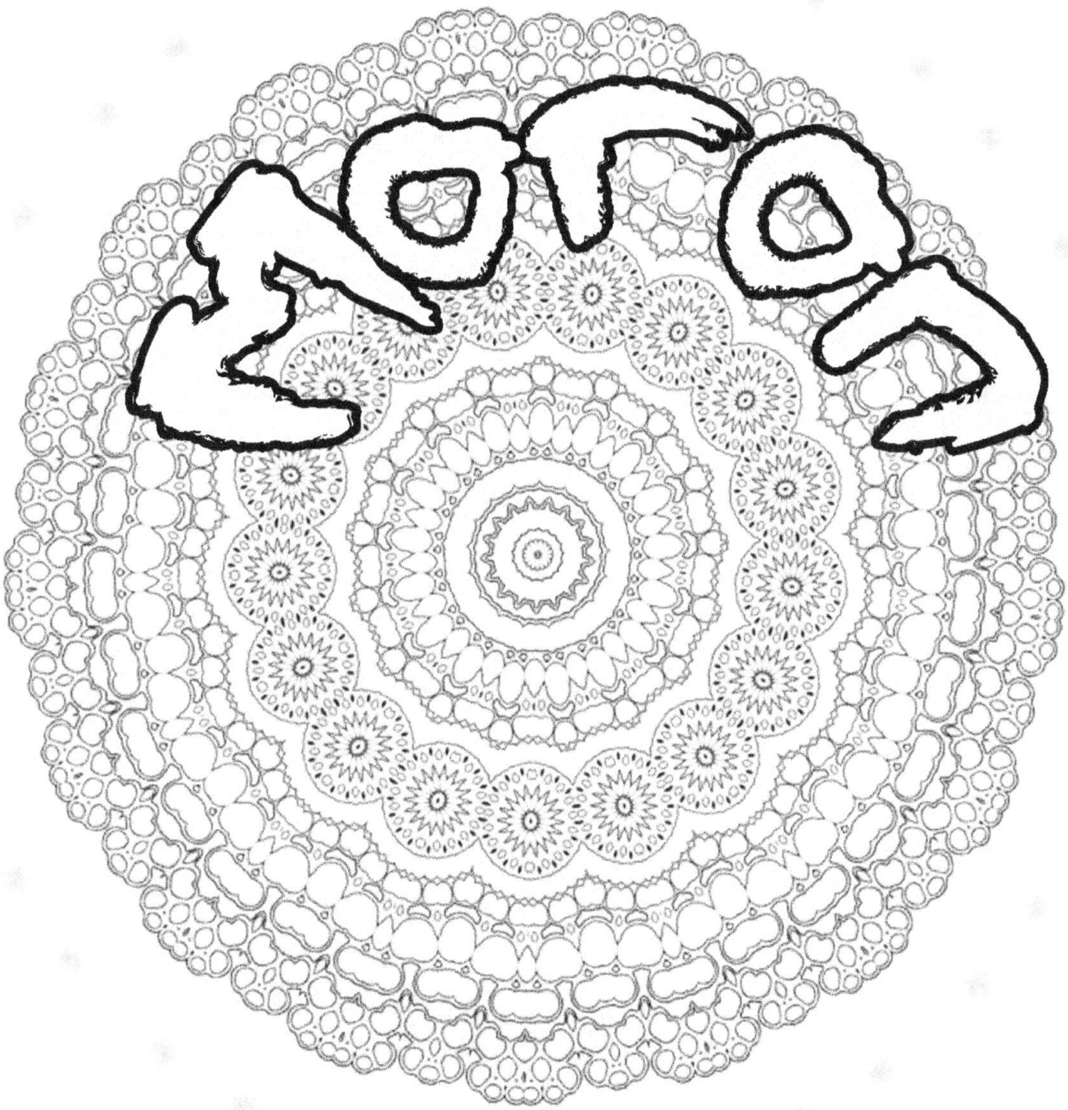
moron

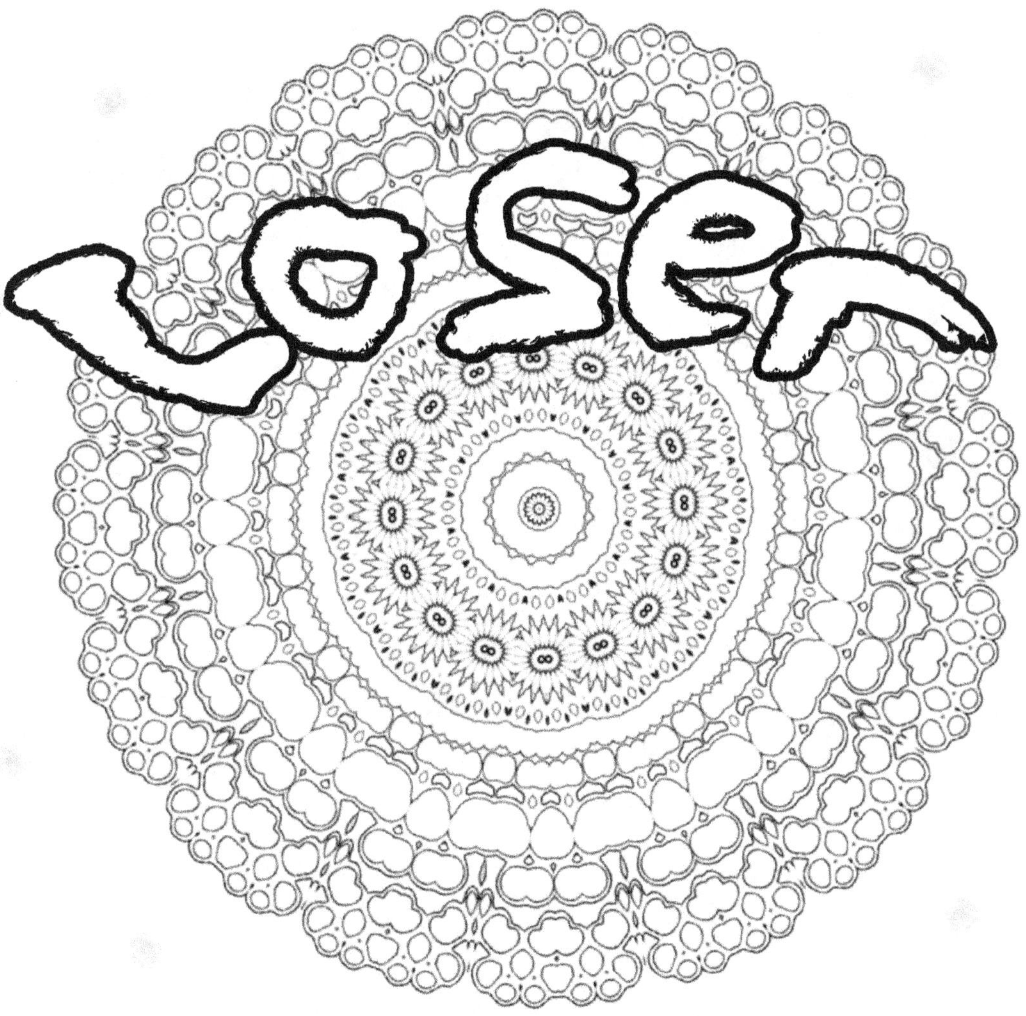
Loser

www.ingramcontent.com/pod-product-compliance
Lightning Source LLC
Chambersburg PA
CBHW081750170526
45167CB00009B/3986
* 9 7 8 1 5 4 4 0 6 2 0 3 7 *